DENTISTS

BY EMMA LESS

AMICUS READERS ● AMICUS INK

amicus
readers

Amicus Readers and Amicus Ink are imprints of Amicus
P.O. Box 1329, Mankato, MN 56002
www.amicuspublishing.us

Cataloging-in-Publication Data is on file with the Library of Congress.
ISBN 978-1-68151-292-1 (library binding)
ISBN 978-1-68152-274-6 (paperback)
ISBN 978-1-68151-354-6 (eBook)

Editor: Valerie Bodden
Designer: Patty Kelley

Photo Credits:
Cover: Michael Zhang/Dreamstime.com
Inside: Dreamstime.com: Monkey Business Images 3, 12, Lopolo 5, Dmitry Shironosov 6, Rozenn Leard 8, Cenkay Sahinalp 11, Evgeniy Kalinovsky 15, Mohamed Osama 16T, Adam Radosavljevic 16R, Imaengine 16B.

Printed in China.

HC 10 9 8 7 6 5 4 3 2 1
PB 10 9 8 7 6 5 4 3 2 1

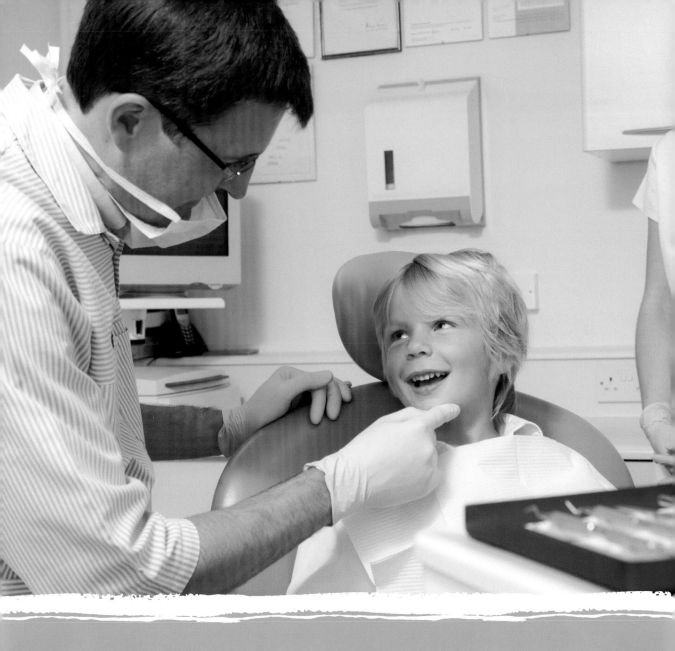

The dentist takes care of teeth.
They are busy!

He wears a mask
and gloves.
These block germs.

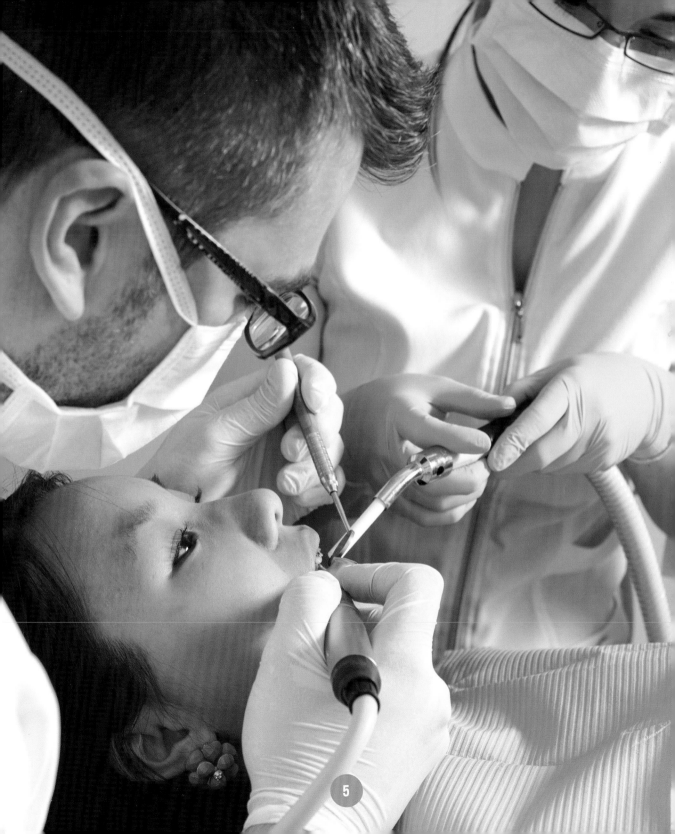

He checks
Ann's teeth.
He uses a pick.
It scrapes bits
of food.

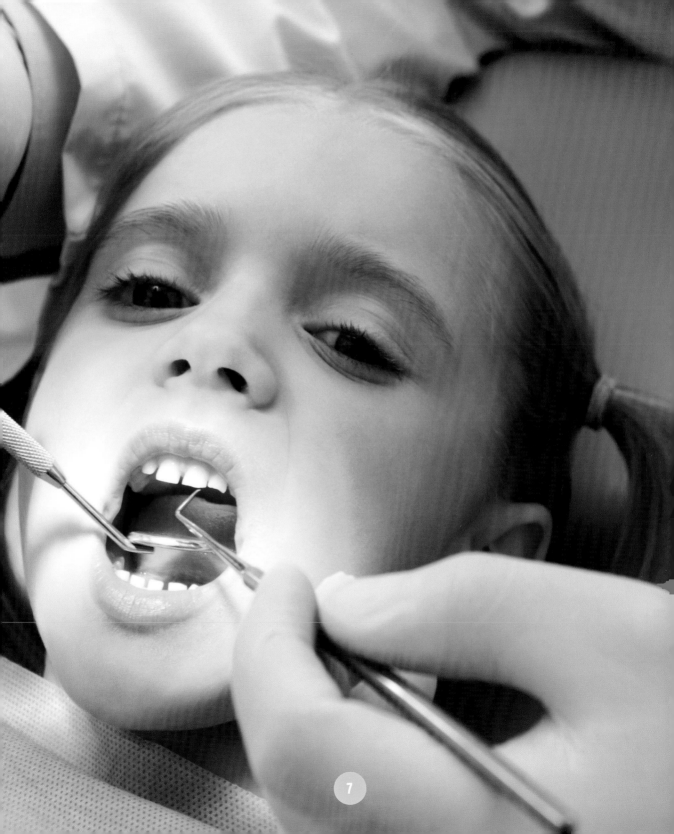

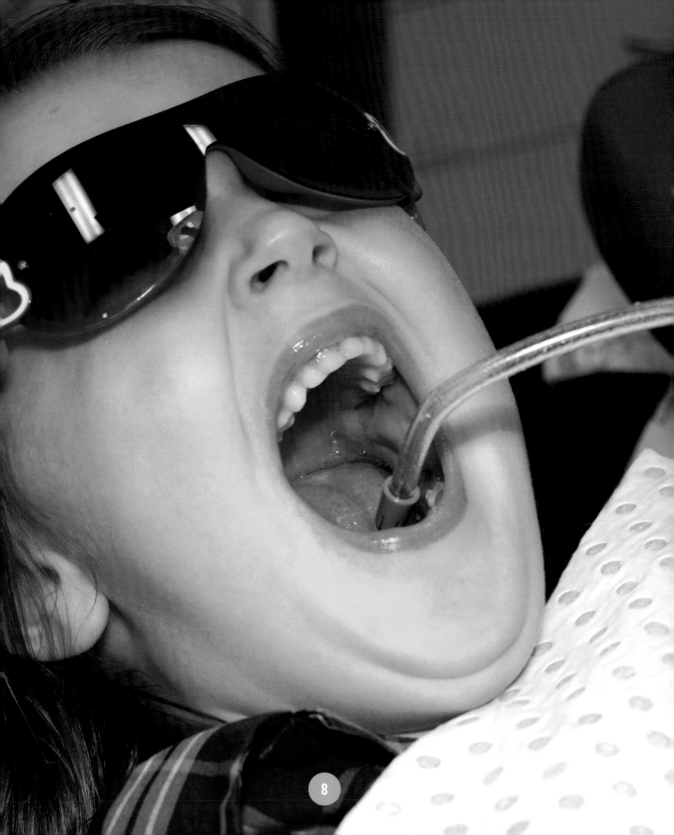

He cleans
May's teeth.
He sprays water
in her mouth.

Tim has a cavity.
He needs it filled.

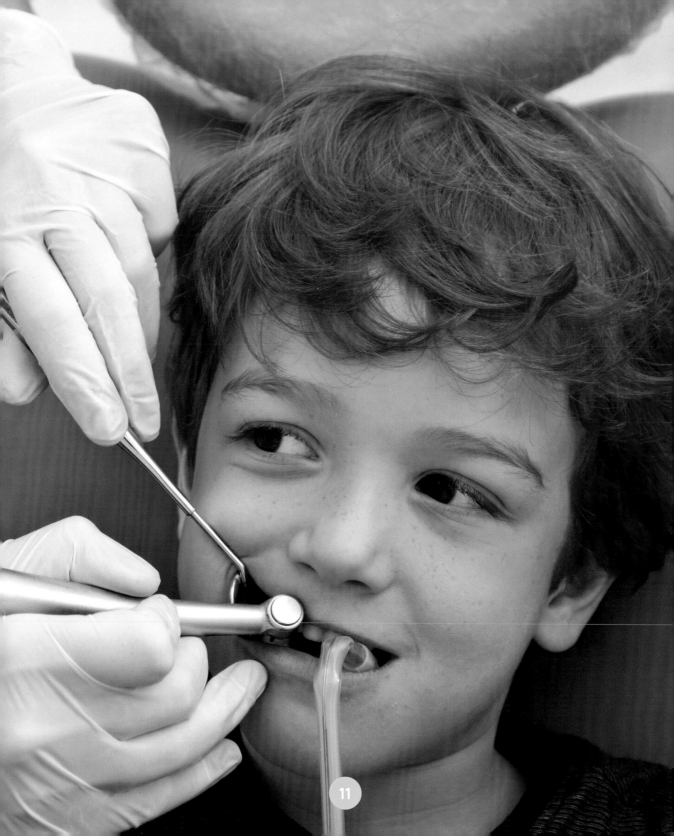

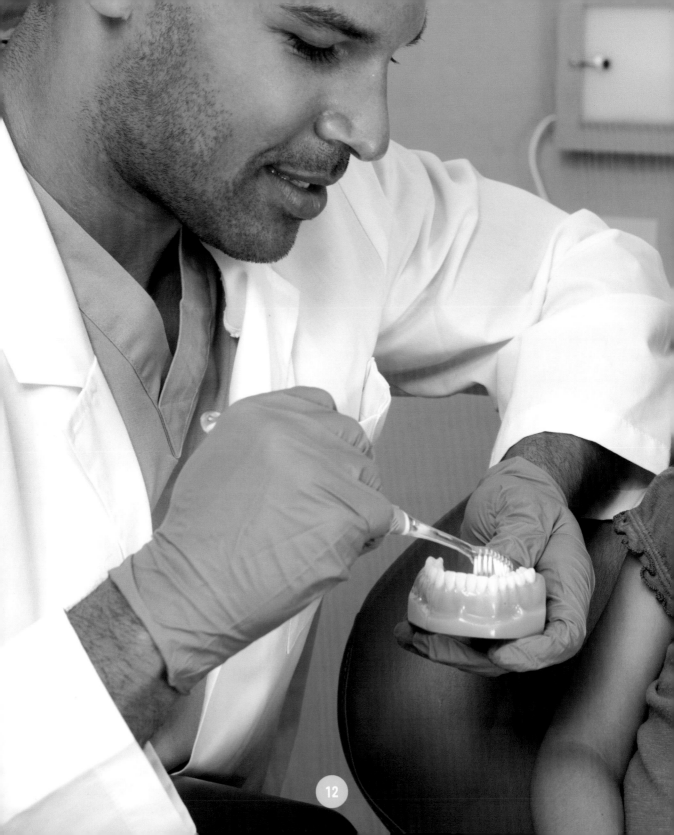

Katie watches
how to brush.
Up and down!
Back and forth!

Keep your
teeth healthy!
Look at that
bright smile!

SEEN AT THE DENTIST'S OFFICE

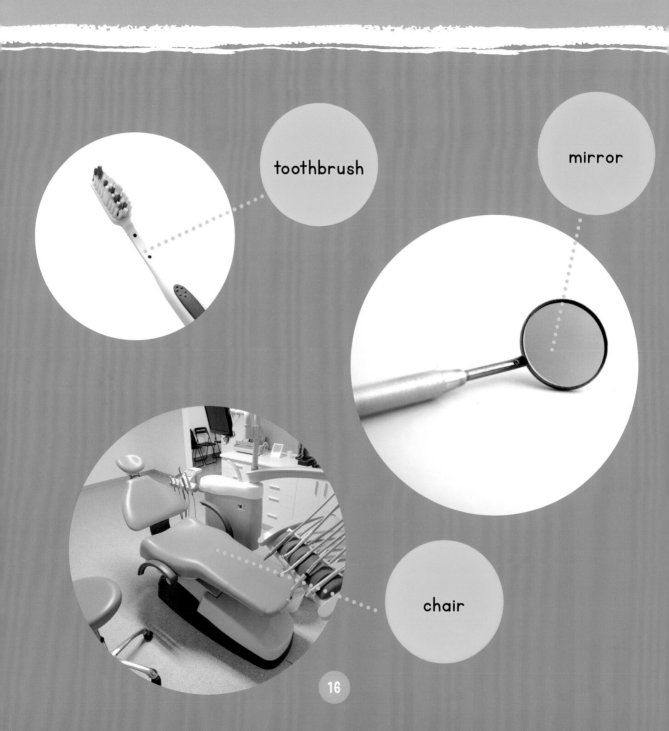

toothbrush

mirror

chair